ᐅᖃᕆᒪᓚᐅᖅᑕᕋ

THE WHITE STRIPES
UNDER GREAT WHITE NORTHERN LIGHTS

PHOTOGRAPHS BY AUTUMN DE WILDE

FOREWORD BY JIM JARMUSCH

CHRONICLE BOOKS

SAN FRANCISCO

FOREWORD

This book of Autumn de Wilde's photographs, *The White Stripes: Under Great White Northern Lights*, is the companion to the film of the same title (or vice versa). Both are documents of The White Stripes' 2007 tour of "every province and territory in Canada," supporting their album *Icky Thump*. But I guess if you're now holding this book, you already know all that . . .

It's interesting to me how both of these documents are made from the same genetic materials: the odd and unusual tour by the band; the uncontained spirit of The White Stripes; their visual style; their strikingly limited range of colors; the haunting qualities of the locations and venues; the distinct personalities of Meg and Jack, with their perfectly balanced yin-yang/boy-girl/sister-brother archetype; and of course their music, which underlies everything.

Somehow though, like Meg and Jack themselves, these two documents form their own yin-yang relationship. The obvious difference is that Emmett Malloy's film is made of movement, sound, and light, while Autumn de Wilde's photographs are made of stillness, silence, and light. But the greater difference is a result of perspective and all the subtle qualities that determine it. I get a strong and exciting sense from this book that these photographs could not have been made by anyone else.

I've never met Autumn de Wilde, but her work, in some almost dreamlike way, has been entering my consciousness for some time now. The images she captures (or creates) have an exquisite way of losing interest in the "realism" innate in their creation. Reality is a reference point for our dreams, but they only really resonate when our subconscious colors outside the lines. The White Stripes can do this with their music. Autumn de Wilde does it with her images. Minor details become portals, but it happens without being forced, and the elegant strangeness of her perceptions also has no interest in calling attention to itself.

So in your hands you have Autumn de Wilde's document of The White Stripes' great Canadian journey. There is Meg, and Jack, there are airplanes and old cars, bizarre landscapes, bowling alleys and fishing boats, equipment cases and cables, dressing rooms and stages, red and white, drums and guitars . . . There are shades of things that could not be caught with a movie camera, shades that maybe only Autumn de Wilde can see—maybe only through the lens of her old-school camera loaded with magical film.

—Jim Jarmusch

PHOTOGRAPHER'S NOTE

Iqaluit.

Looking down through the windows of the plane, we saw it.
One school, one hotel, a hockey rink, a playground, and a graveyard.
A scattering of homes and a white house with two red doors.
No trees, just the mythical tundra, ice, and water.
The tide was in. It was summer, but the ice never completely melts around here, so the water swelled around the floating pieces.

Jack and Meg had brought us here.

I placed my finger on a map and drew an imaginary line with my finger from Iqaluit to the tip of Greenland. We were that far north. I looked at the mysterious curved line at the top of the map as I had when I was a little girl in Los Angeles and touched the words *Arctic Circle*. I certainly was closer to it than I ever thought I would be.

Thirty-three black suits, red ties, and black hats stared out the window.

The beautiful city of Vancouver, the lush green trees of Whitehorse, and the stories told by the Snow King of Yellowknife were behind us now. There were free shows to come, on a bus and on a boat; flags of each province to wave; and on July 14 in Glace Bay, Nova Scotia, Jack and Meg would waltz as the bagpipes sang at the close of their tenth-anniversary show. Our civilian lives would resume after the first-ever, one-note show and Jack's announcement that The White Stripes had now played every province and territory in Canada.

As we landed in Iqaluit, Emmett Malloy readied his small film crew, I reloaded my camera with film, Jack and Meg rose from their seats, and we all acknowledged that this cyclone carrying The White Stripes had taken us far, far away from the things we thought we knew.

The good people of Iqaluit welcomed the citizens of black, white, and red (plus one Jack and one Meg) as we stepped onto the wet tarmac. No tours had ever come this far, and we all raised a glass to the spirit of adventure.

We visited the graveyard where every summer, ten graves are dug in preparation for the eight months of the year when the ice has no mercy. The dead are covered by rocks until ground can be broken again the following summer. We paid our respects and afterwards sat with the Innuit elders in their meeting place. They shared their food, and Jack and Meg played music with them. Dust stirred on the dance floor. The elders spoke of the wisdom of crows and told us of the old ways of the Innuit before wood, plastic, and cars changed their landscape forever.

Meanwhile, lights were borrowed from the school theatre, a stage was erected, and ninety-nine pounds of red fabric billowed down from a rail suspended across the ceiling of a hockey rink.

The show.

Young and old gathered. Some knew the band well, and some knew nothing of this band called The White Stripes. The energy was electric. A brother and a sister began to play, and a lightning bolt of red, black, and white struck down between them, and then it was over. At 12:33 a.m., Jack and Meg walked out into the permanent twilight, shook hands, and stared out at the landscape that had welcomed them. We returned to the hotel to fall into our beds, but some of us couldn't sleep. Still wearing my black suit, red tie, and black hat, I walked with my camera down to the beach in the white northern night with another of my brothers. The show was on our lips as we walked toward the ice and sand. The fog was thick and the night was quiet. I heard something. We stopped and listened. "That little shack way over there on the beach," he said. "It's coming from there." We crept closer and heard the black sound of a yearning guitar, then the blood-red heartbeat of a desperate base drum, and finally a white-hot howling voice joined their ranks. At three in the morning on the edge of the world, a citizen of Iqaluit was blasting "Seven Nation Army" as loud as they could inside a nine-foot shack built of plywood.

—Autumn de Wilde

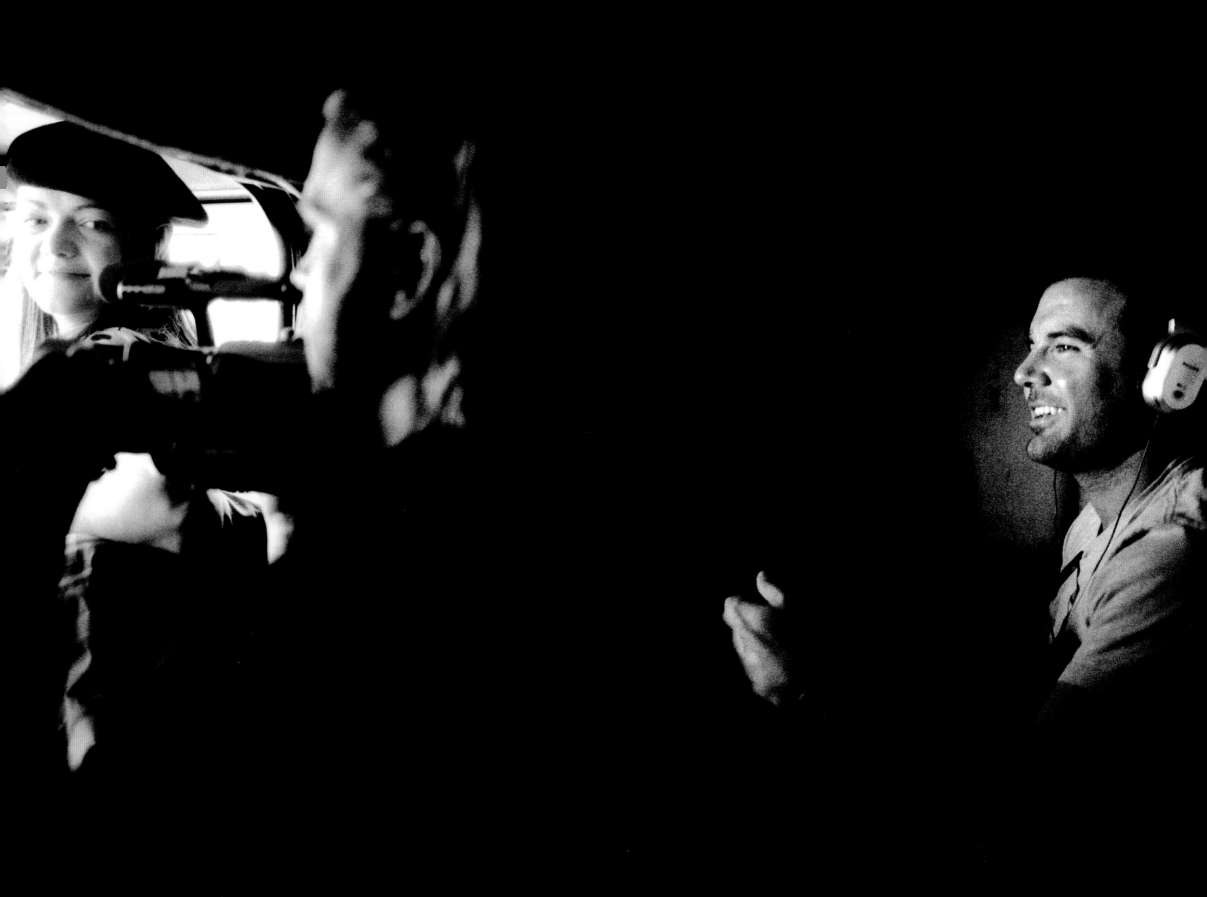

THE WHITE STRIPES

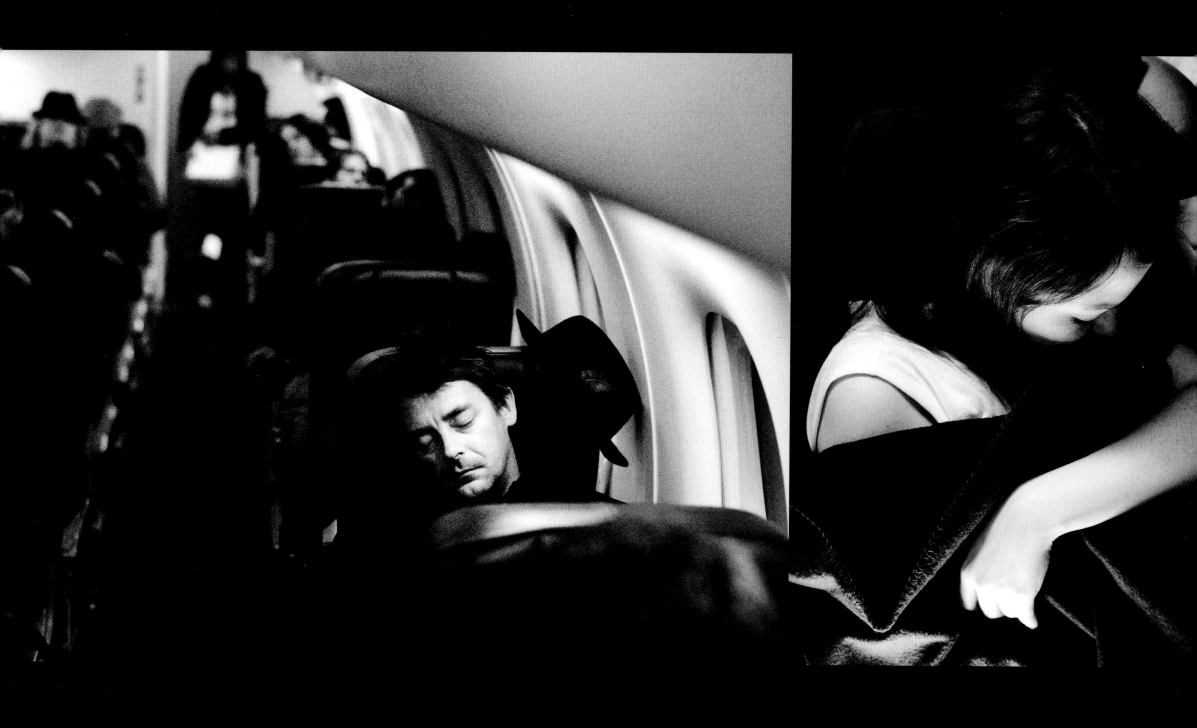

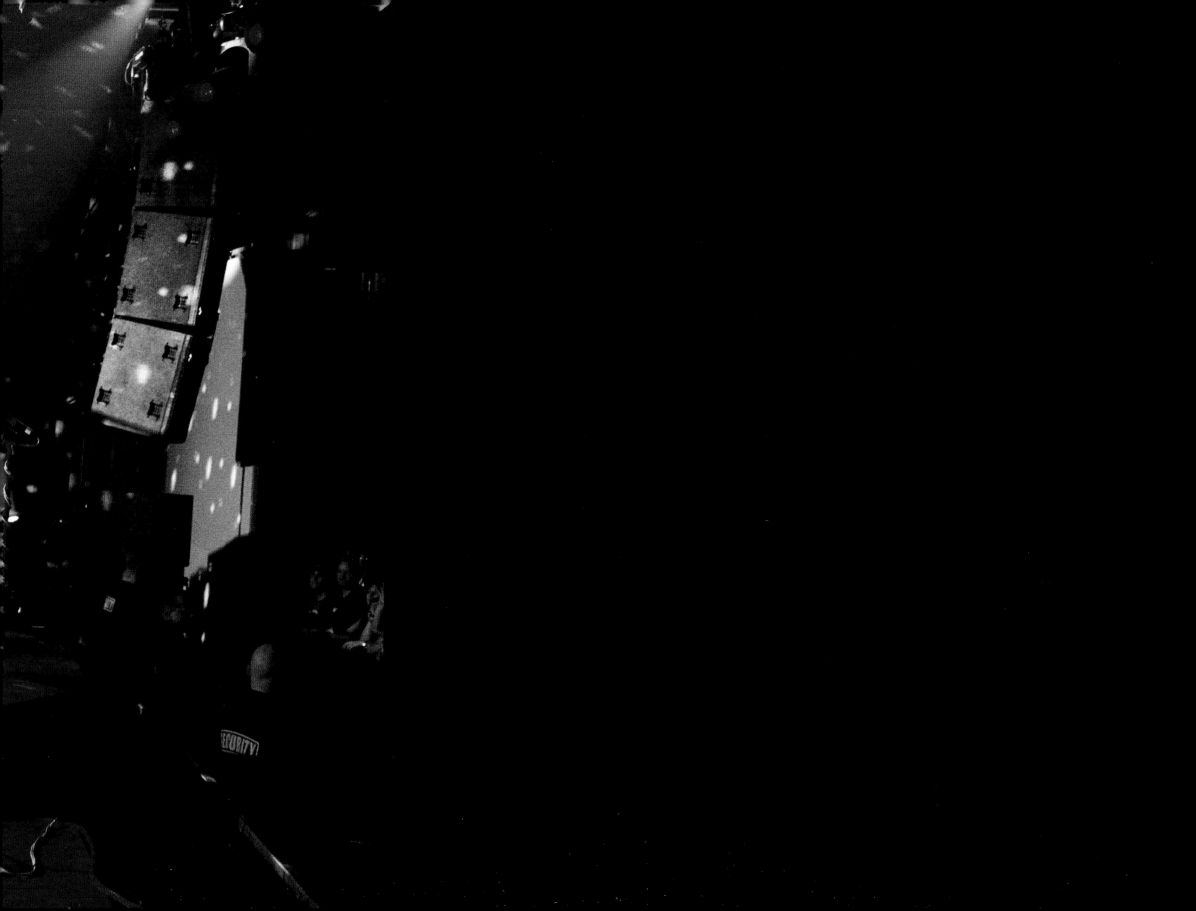

ALUMINUM
ANNIVERSARY
SHOW POSTER
PRINTED ON ALUMINUM!!!
$75

THE WHITE STRIPES   07 14 07   ASHLEY MacISSAC and DAN SARTAIN   SAVOY THEATRE   GLACE BAY, NOVA SCOTIA

ISBN: 978-0-8118-7223-2

Library of Congress Cataloging-in-Publication data available.

Manufactured in the United States of America.

Design by Jeri Heiden, SMOG Design, Inc.
Cover and map design by Rob Jones at Animal Rummy.
Silver gelatin prints and C prints by Schulman Photo Lab, Los Angeles, CA.
Photographic print production overseen by Meghan Gallagher, studio manager for Autumn de Wilde.
Color separations and printing by Shapco Printing, Minneapolis, MN.

10 9 8 7 6 5 4 3 2 1

Chronicle Books LLC
680 Second Street
San Francisco, California 94107

www.chroniclebooks.com